NATIONAL GEOGRAPHIC

Fall Colors

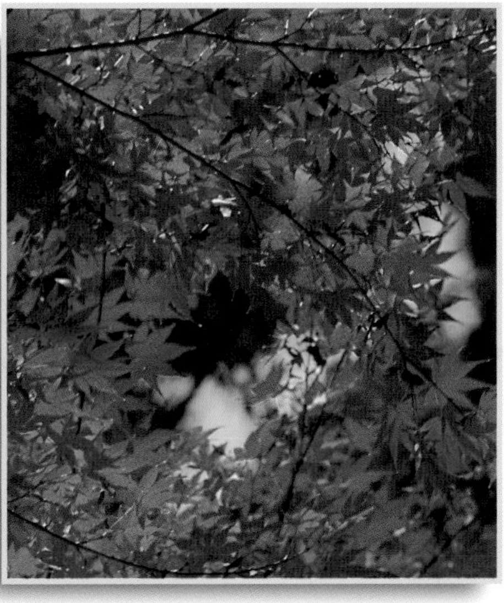

Santina Bruni

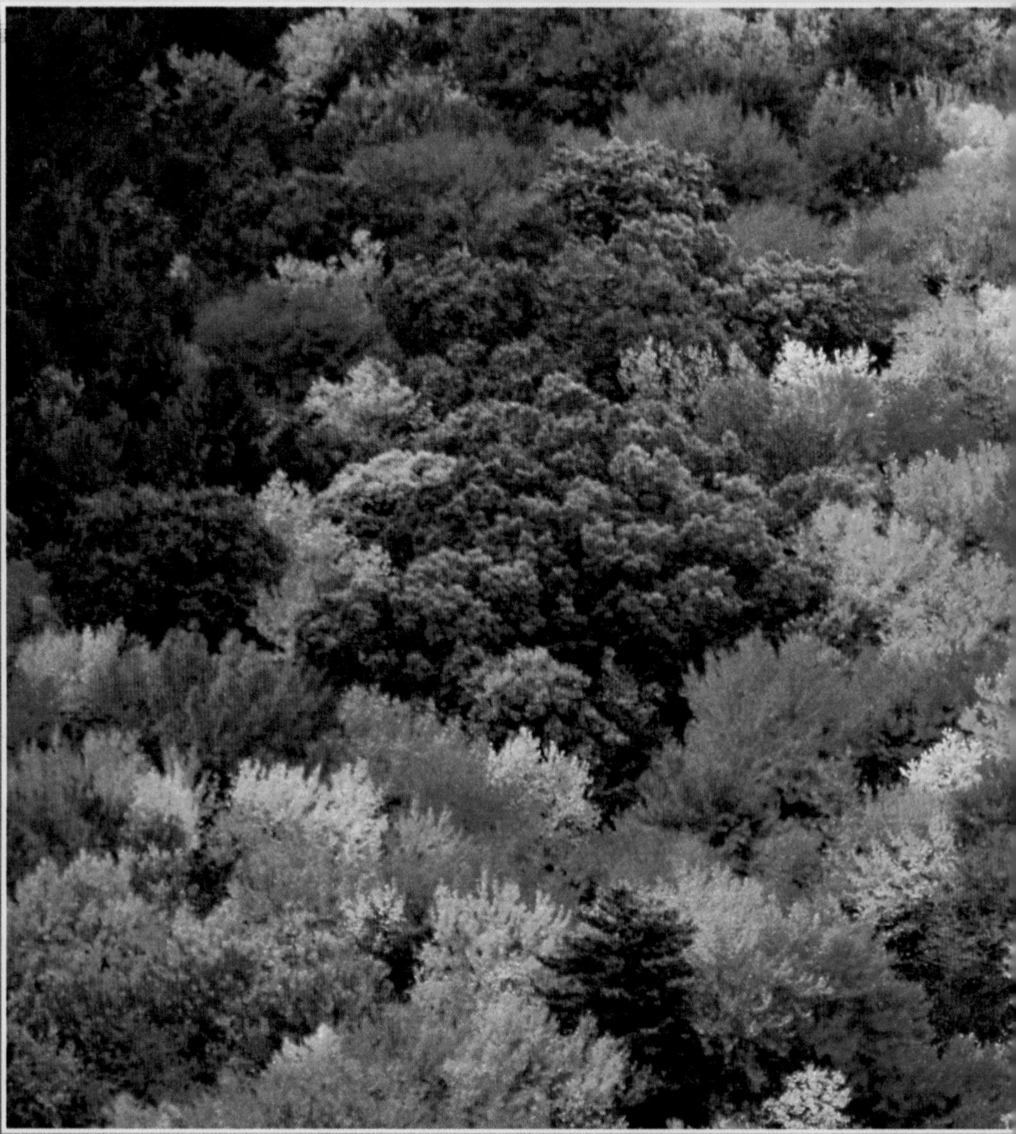

Leaves change colo

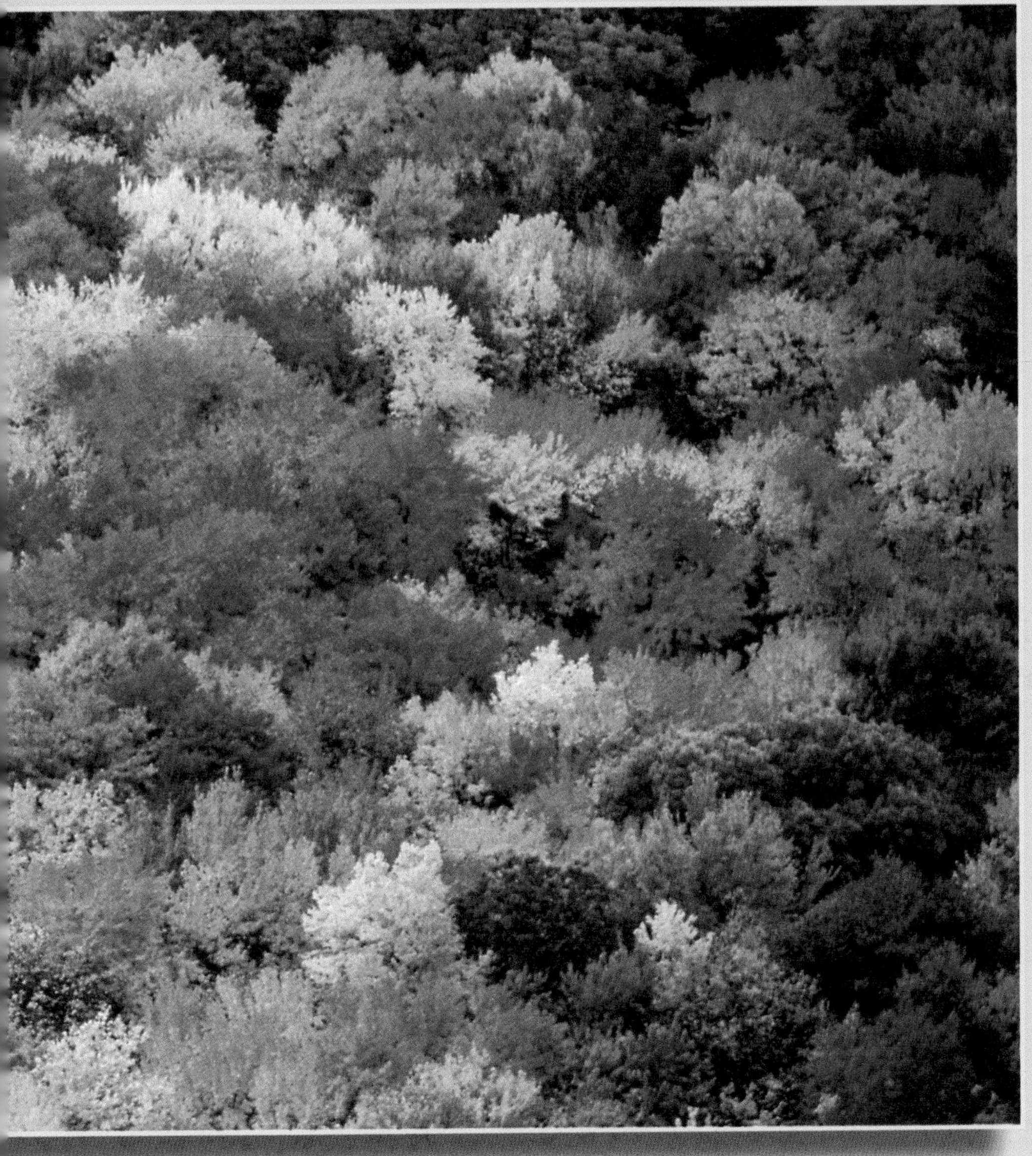

in the fall.

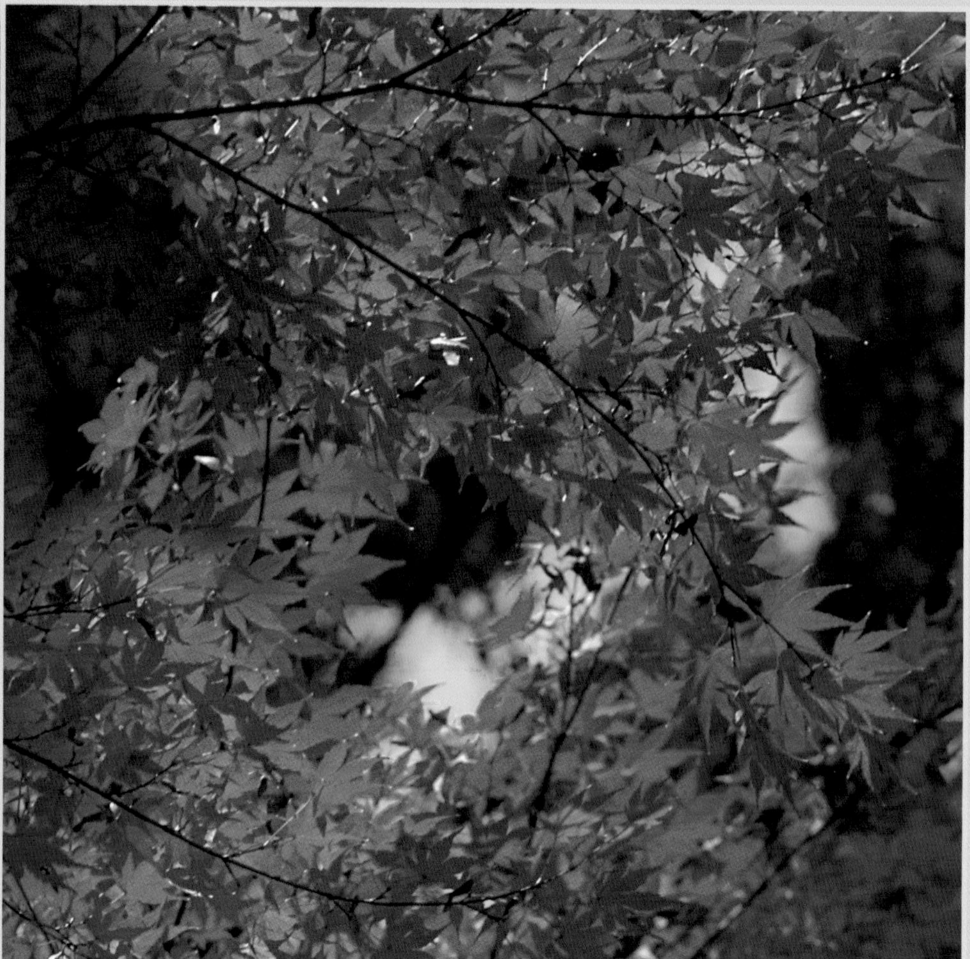

red leaves

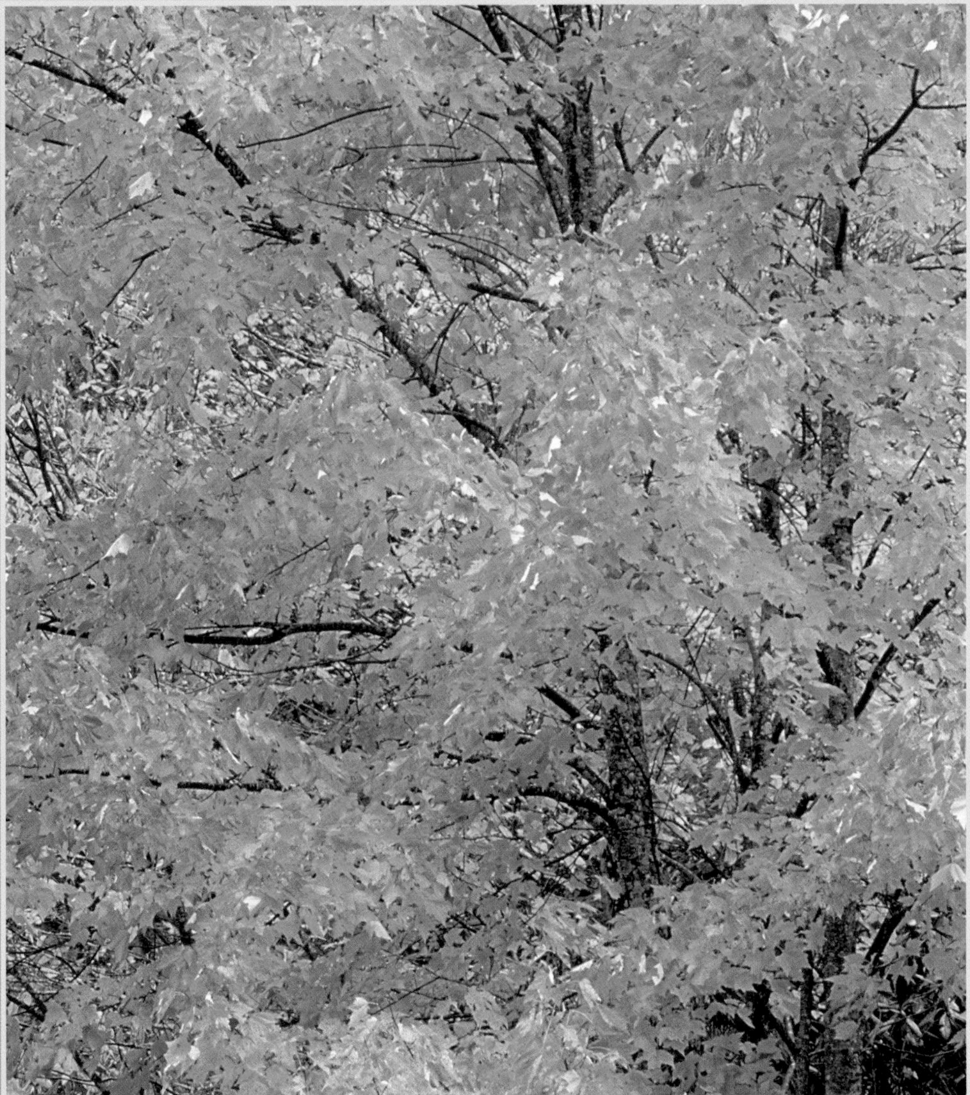

orange leaves

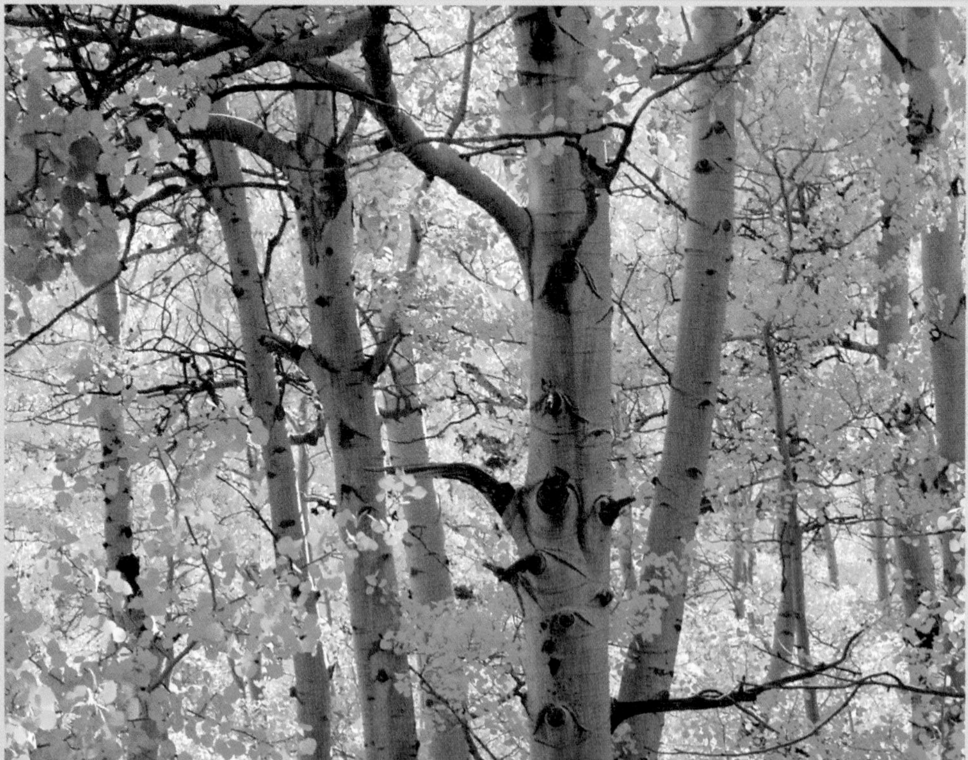

yellow leaves

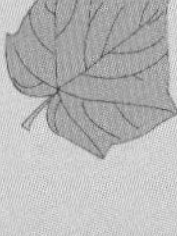

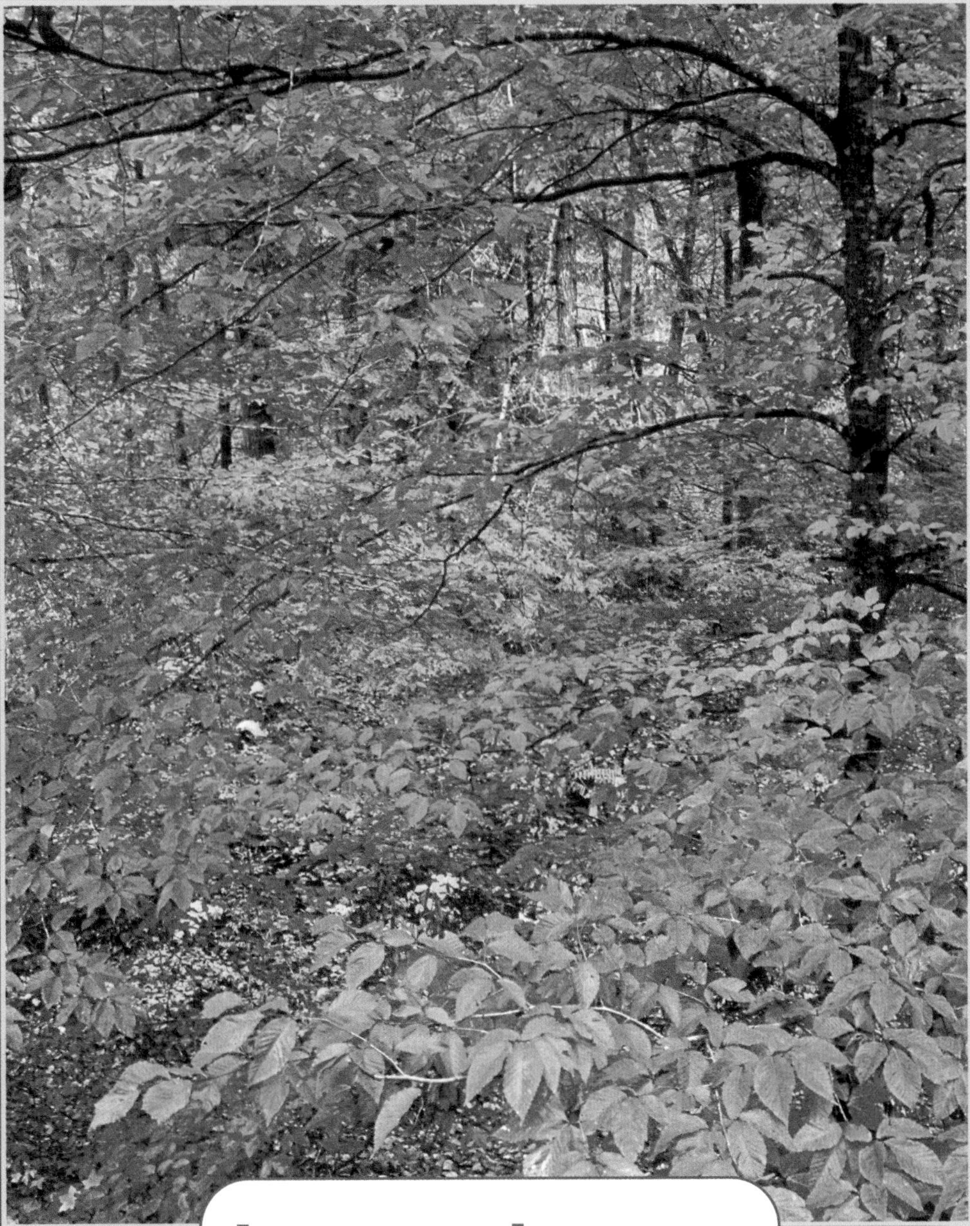

brown leaves

What colors are fall leaves?

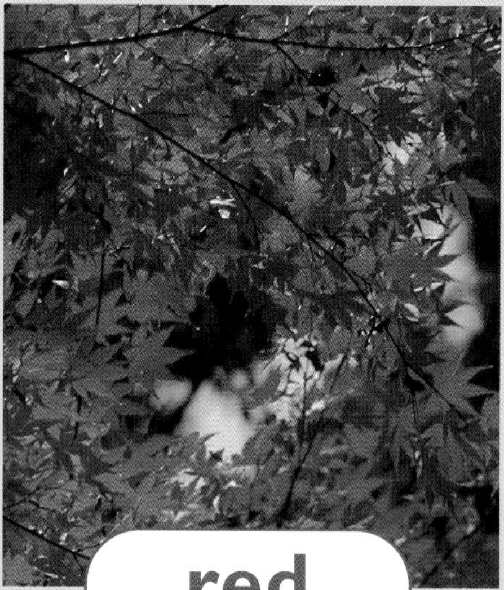

red

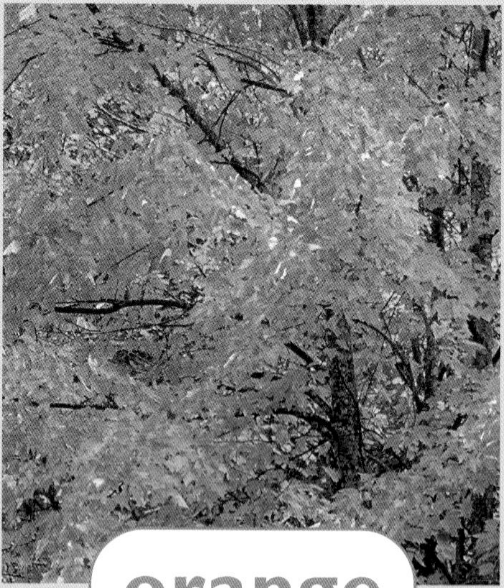

orange

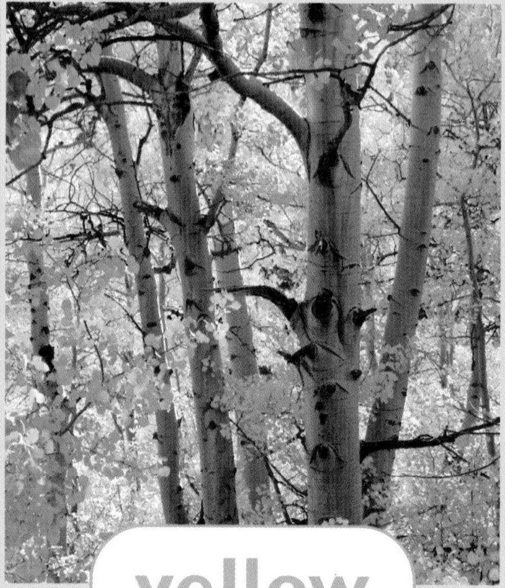

yellow

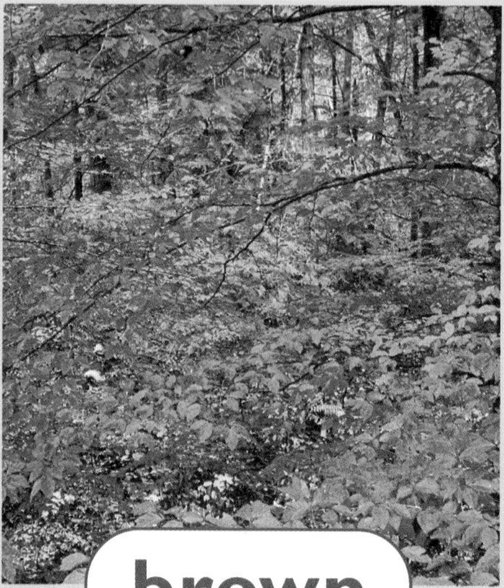

brown